St. Helena Library

P9-BIC-591

JAPANESE IMMIGRANTS

1850-1950

by Rosemary Wallner

Content Consultant:
Rosalyn Tonai, Executive Director
National Japanese American Historical Society
San Francisco, California

Blue Earth Books

an imprint of Capstone Press
Mankato, Minnesota

Blue Earth Books are published by Capstone Press
151 Good Counsel Drive, P.O. Box 669, Mankato, Minnesota 56002
http://www.capstone-press.com

Library of Congress Cataloging-in-Publication Data
Wallner, Rosemary, 1964–
    Japanese immigrants, 1850–1950 / by Rosemary Wallner.
    p. cm. — (Coming to America)
    Includes bibliographical references (p. 31) and index.
    ISBN 0-7368-0797-7
    1. Japanese Americans—History—Juvenile literature. 2. Immigrants—United States—History—Juvenile literature. 3. United States—
Emigration and immigration—History—Juvenile literature. 4. Japan—Emigration and immigration—History—Juvenile literature. [1. Japanese
Americans—History. 2. Immigrants—History. 3. United States—Emigration and immigration.] I. Title II. Coming to America (Mankato, Minn.)
    E184.J3 W25 2002
    973' .04956—dc21   2001000732

Summary: Discusses the reasons Japanese people left their homeland to come to America, the experiences immigrants had in the new country, and the contributions this cultural group made to American society. Includes sidebars and activities.

Editorial credits
Editor: Kay M. Olson
Designer: Heather Kindseth
Photo Researchers: Heidi Schoof and Alta Schaffer
Product Planning Editor: Lois Wallentine

Photo credits
National Archives, cover, 13, 22, 23; Bishop Museum, 4, 14, 15 (left); Gregg Andersen, flag images; Library of Congress, 6, 8, 19; Bettmann/CORBIS, 7 (right), 10, 11; CORBIS, 7 (left), 12; Asian Art & Archaeology, Inc./CORBIS, 9; Artville/Jeff Burke and Lorraine Triolo, 15 (right); Denver Public Library, Western History Collection, 16, 21; The Bancroft Library, University of California, Berkeley, 17; National Archives and Records Administration—Pacific Region (San Francisco), 20; Capstone Press/Gary Sundermeyer, 24, 25, 26; ALLSPORT PHOTOGRAPHY, 29 (bottom); Reuters Newmedia, Inc./CORBIS, 29 (top)

1 2 3 4 5 6 07 06 05 04 03 02

Contents

JAPANESE IMMIGRANTS 1850 TO 1950

EARLY JAPANESE IMMIGRANTS

The first Japanese immigrants who traveled to Hawaii were mostly poor, young men looking for adventure. They also wanted to work and learn about a new culture.

In the 1600s, Japan did not allow foreigners into the country. Some European explorers tried to stop in Japanese ports, but they were not allowed to stay. Japanese people were ruled by shogun and emperors. These leaders made laws to keep Japanese citizens in Japan.

In 1868, Japan's young emperor, Meji, allowed representatives from foreign countries to visit Japan. Emperor Meji also allowed the first Japanese emigrants to leave the country. These people went to Hawaii to work on the sugarcane and pineapple plantations. During the next 40 years, more than 150,000 Japanese workers sailed to Hawaii.

Between 1885 and 1898, about 45,000 Japanese sailed to Hawaii. By the end of the century, Japanese immigrants made up 80 percent of Hawaii's labor force. Some Japanese immigrants sailed farther east to the U.S. mainland. Farmers and railroad builders needed workers in the western United States. Japanese immigration to the U.S. mainland continued to grow after Hawaii became a U.S. territory in 1898.

By the early 1900s, the Japanese government began to limit the number of people allowed to go to the United States. During the next 30 years, Japanese immigration to America decreased by one-third. Japanese immigration stopped entirely during World War II (1939–1945).

Today, about 850,000 people in the United States are of Japanese descent. Hawaii has the largest number of Japanese Americans. More than 20 percent of the population of Hawaii's Oahu Island have Japanese ancestors.

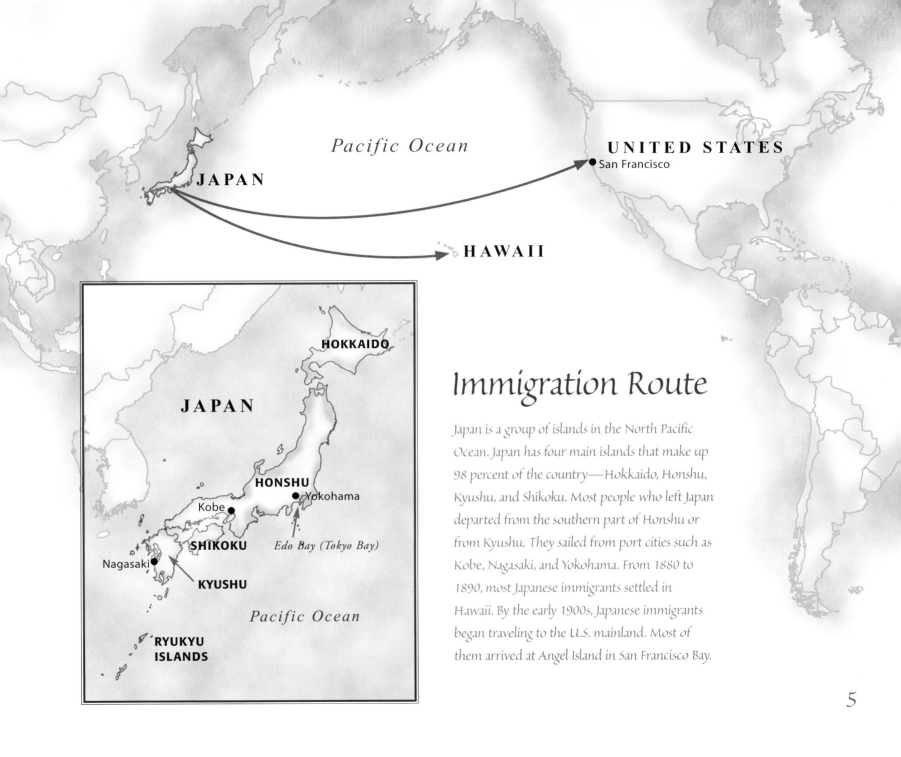

Pacific Ocean

JAPAN

UNITED STATES
● San Francisco

HAWAII

HOKKAIDO

JAPAN

HONSHU
Kobe ●
● Yokohama

SHIKOKU
Edo Bay (Tokyo Bay)

Nagasaki ●

KYUSHU

Pacific Ocean

RYUKYU
ISLANDS

Immigration Route

Japan is a group of islands in the North Pacific Ocean. Japan has four main islands that make up 98 percent of the country—Hokkaido, Honshu, Kyushu, and Shikoku. Most people who left Japan departed from the southern part of Honshu or from Kyushu. They sailed from port cities such as Kobe, Nagasaki, and Yokohama. From 1880 to 1890, most Japanese immigrants settled in Hawaii. By the early 1900s, Japanese immigrants began traveling to the U.S. mainland. Most of them arrived at Angel Island in San Francisco Bay.

5

LIFE IN THE OLD COUNTRY

Most Japanese farm families grew rice. Farmers used rice to pay their debts as well as to feed their families.

In the 1600s, the Japanese people were divided into four classes—samurai warriors, farmers, craftspeople, and traders. Some people did not fit into this tight class system. They included actors, poets, priests, and eta. The eta were outcasts who handled all work involving the death of people or animals. Eta buried the dead, butchered livestock, and tanned animal hides.

Samurai warriors were the most respected class in Japan. These soldiers held great power. The shogun ruled the samurai and gave orders to the daimyo, who were local landowners. Each daimyo had an army of samurai to keep order over the land.

Farmers were the next most respected class. Their lives were filled with hard work. Japanese farmers grew rice, which required much physical labor. The shogun took part of the rice harvest and gave shares of it to the daimyo. Farmers kept what was left of the rice, sometimes less than half of the crop.

Craftspeople and traders were separate classes, but their work sometimes was similar. Cloth makers, carpenters, and sword makers made goods and often sold them as well. Traders were at the bottom of Japanese society because they did not make anything. They earned money from the labor of others.

This class system continued unchanged in Japan for hundreds of years. Sons took on the same occupations as their fathers. Families continued to live and work in the same social class generation after generation. Government leaders wanted the people to follow Japanese customs. They wanted to keep Western visitors out of Japan to prevent Japanese people from following Western ways.

In 1853, the Japanese received a visitor that changed their way of life. Commodore Matthew Perry sailed into Edo Bay, which today is known as Tokyo Bay. Perry was a commodore in the U.S. Navy. He sailed with a fleet of American gunships. Perry demanded that Japan allow his crew and other foreigners into their country.

Commodore Matthew Perry (right) and his crew sailed to Japan in 1853. Some of Perry's sailors (shown above) visited the people and villages of Japan's Ryukyu Islands. Perry and his crew were the first Americans to visit Japan.

7

Japanese women often carried babies in baskets hanging from a yoke. Grandmothers assigned duties such as cooking and cleaning to the women of their families.

In the late 1800s and early 1900s, the Japanese government increased trade with other countries and built up its military. Japanese officials encouraged people to travel to the United States and the Hawaiian Territory.

Throughout this time of change, the Japanese people still held onto their customs. Generations of a single family often lived together in the same home. The head of the household usually was the grandfather or his eldest married son.

By the late 1800s, thousands of Japanese people began to leave the country. Many men left Japan to earn money. They wanted to help their families get out of debt and start a new life. In Japan, farms were passed to the eldest son when the father died. The family's younger sons had no land of their own and few skills other than farming. Many of these second sons left Japan looking for adventure or for ways to earn money.

Some Japanese people wanted to leave their homeland for other reasons. All Japanese men between the ages of 20 and 32 were required to serve in the army. Some men left Japan to avoid their military duty. Others wanted to escape the strict Japanese class structure. People who had broken the law sometimes left Japan to avoid going to prison.

Most people departed Japan from the southern part of Honshu or from Kyushu. Many traveled eastward to Hawaii to work on sugarcane and pineapple plantations. Others traveled farther east to the United States in search of gold or a job.

★ Writing Haiku ★

Poets were among the few people in Japan who did not belong to a strict social class. Japanese poets often wrote in a traditional verse form called haiku. This poetry style began in the 1500s and continues today. Haiku always is about a single topic.

What You Need

paper

pencil

What You Do

First, think of a subject and narrow that subject down to a simple idea. You may decide to write a haiku about your best friend. Narrow down the subject to your friend's smile. Or focus on a tiny detail of where you live.

A haiku does not have to rhyme or be a complete sentence. Each haiku has a total of 17 syllables, or units of sound. The first and third lines each have five syllables. The second line has seven syllables. These two haiku poems may give you ideas to write your own.

Basho was Japan's most famous haiku poet. He lived from 1644 to 1694. Basho traveled all over Japan. He often wrote about his experiences in haiku verse.

My Friend's Smile

Shin—y — teeth — gleam—ing	(5 syllables)
Be—hind — sil—ver — lines — of — wire	(7 syllables)
Ash—ley — grins — at — me.	(5 syllables)

The Road to My House

Curv—ing — ce—ment — path	(5 syllables)
Smooth — sur—face — with — spi—der — lines	(7 syllables)
A — fresh — drive—way — crack.	(5 syllables)

THE TRIP OVER

Immigrant children who had been born in Japan were not allowed U.S. citizenship. But their younger brothers and sisters born in America were U.S. citizens.

In the late 1800s, Japanese people applied for a permit if they wanted to emigrate, or leave the country. They went to an official in the district where they lived. The official asked questions about each person's family, education, and health. The Japanese government wanted to be sure emigrants were healthy, intelligent people who would be good representatives of Japan.

Officials had heard that Americans unfairly judged or discriminated against people from other countries. They knew that some Americans mistreated the uneducated and poor Chinese immigrants who had settled on the West Coast. Japanese officials thought that if Japanese emigrants were well-educated people, Americans would not discriminate against them.

The Japanese government encouraged wives and children to leave the country with their husbands and fathers. Officials believed that Japanese men would work harder if they had their families with them. But most of the people who first decided to emigrate were young single men and a few young single women. Some Japanese emigrants were teenagers.

After government officials approved the permits, emigrants had to find the money to pay for their steamship tickets. Hawaiian labor contractors and landowners paid the boat passage for some groups of emigrants. These people worked off the price of their ticket before they began to earn wages. Others had to pay for the trip themselves. They often borrowed money from lenders and promised to pay it back with their new wages. If they did not pay back the money, the lenders could take their land in Japan as payment.

With a permit to leave and a boat passage ticket, Japanese emigrants began the journey to Hawaii and the U.S. mainland. Most traveled to one of Japan's three major port cities. They went to the cities of Yokohama or Kobe on the island of Honshu. Other Japanese emigrants traveled to Nagasaki in western Kyushu.

At the port cities, emigrants had to pass a health exam. Officials checked them to make sure they had no diseases. An American doctor usually inspected them too. Those who passed the health exam could board the ship.

The future was uncertain for the emigrants. They did not know when they would return to their homeland. Many thought they would be back in a few years, after they had earned enough money to pay their debts and help their families. Others left with their families hoping to build a new life in a new place.

The emigrants did not take much with them on their journey. Usually they packed clothes and personal items such as photographs. They also brought wicker baskets with rice, noodles, and dried fish to eat on the voyage.

In the early 1900s, many women and children traveled to America to join their husbands and fathers.

U.S. officials sometimes met arriving immigrants on board the ship. The immigrants had to pass a health exam and receive immunization shots before they could enter the United States.

From the ports of Japan, the emigrants traveled more than 4,000 miles (6,400 kilometers) across the Pacific Ocean to Hawaii. The voyage lasted about 10 days. The trip from Hawaii to the U.S. mainland was another 2,300 miles (3,700 kilometers).

The emigrants crossed the Pacific Ocean in large steamships. Most bought third-class tickets and were crowded together in the lower parts of the ship. Each third-class passenger usually received a small bunk or hammock. Men and women slept in separate parts of the ship. Children often slept with their mothers.

Traveling aboard the ship was not pleasant. Many travelers had never been on a large ship for a long period of time. They often became seasick. Passengers used buckets for toilets. The air smelled of human sweat and waste.

The weather sometimes was stormy and the ship tossed and turned in the waves. Some ships had pieces of netting attached to the low ceilings. As the passengers lay in their bunks, they held onto the netting to avoid being tossed on the floor.

There was little to do on the long journey. Many seasick passengers stayed in their bunks most of the day. Others went up on deck for fresh air. They saw nothing but the sky and the ocean. Many hopeful passengers strained their eyes to get the first view of land.

★ Japanese American Generations ★

Japanese Americans have a special name for each generation of a family. Sei (SAY) means "generation" or "an age" and comes at the end of the name for each generation. Is (EES) means "one," so Issei means "first generation." The word "ki" means "to return." Kibei is the word for Japanese Americans born in the United States but raised or educated in Japan and who later return to live in America.

Japanese Americans use the term Issei to describe the first generation of immigrants who went to the United States in the late 1800s. This generation was the first to live outside Japan. The term Nisei describes the Issei's children, the second generation. Many Nisei grew up in the United States in the early to mid-1900s.

Sansei is the term used for the third generation, or children of the Nisei. Sansei are the grandchildren of Issei. Yonsei is the fourth generation and Gosei is the fifth generation. Today, many children of Japanese Americans are Gosei or Rokusei.

Name	Pronounced	Means
Issei	EES-say	first generation
Nisei	NEE-say	second generation
Sansei	SAHN-say	third generation
Yonsei	YOHN-say	fourth generation
Gosei	GOH-say	fifth generation
Rokusei	ROH-KOO-say	sixth generation

ARRIVING IN AMERICA

From 1880 to 1890, most Japanese immigrants traveled to Hawaii. At that time, Hawaii was an independent country ruled by King Kalakaua. Ships usually transported Japanese immigrants to Sand Island. This island became the main Hawaiian entry point for Japanese immigrants.

Labor contractors took new immigrants directly to the plantations to begin working. Plantation workers planted, hoed, weeded, cut, gathered, and hauled crops under the hot sun. Hoe-hana was one of the hardest plantation chores. Workers hoed the land in a straight line for four hours at a time without resting, stretching, straightening their backs, or talking.

In 1885, the Japanese emperor and the Hawaiian king made an official immigration agreement. Both countries allowed more Japanese workers to come to Hawaii as contract laborers on sugarcane plantations. These new immigrants would work without wages for three years to pay off their ship passage and living expenses. About 45,000 Japanese people left their homes for Hawaii during the next 15 years.

Japanese men and women traveled to Hawaii to work as plantation laborers. Men were given the hardest chores. Women workers often worked at a task called hole-hole. They stripped dried cane leaves from the sugar stalks.

In the late 1800s, most Japanese immigrants found jobs working on the many sugarcane (left) and pineapple plantations in Hawaii.

By the 1870s, the United States was growing rapidly and businesses needed laborers. With the promise of jobs, more Japanese immigrants came to the United States. From 1885 to 1899, about 55,000 new Japanese immigrants arrived looking for work.

In 1900, U.S. President William McKinley signed the Organic Act that made Hawaii a U.S. territory. This act also made it illegal for plantation owners to hire people under labor contracts. Japanese immigrants had to pay their own passage. Those who could afford it went to the U.S. mainland, hoping for better working conditions and wages.

15

"I grew up on a farm in Japan. My father owned a fairly large piece of land, but it was heavily mortgaged. I remember how hard we all had to work, and I also remember the hard times. I saw little future in farm work; my older brother would later run the farm, so at my first good chance, I went to work in Osaka. Later I came to California and worked as a laborer in all kinds of jobs. However, for the first five years I had to work in the farms, picking fruit, vegetables and I saved some money. Then I came to live in the city permanently."

—remembrances of an Issei (first-generation) man, 1964

These early Japanese immigrants settled all along the western United States. Some stayed in California while others went to Oregon or Washington. Some even traveled as far north as Alaska. A few others moved to the Midwest.

Japanese plantation laborers who had worked in Hawaii did not find better conditions on the U.S. mainland. Many immigrants could find only low-paying jobs.

Some Japanese immigrants found jobs building railroads across the United States.

Japanese immigrant families began settling near one another. They lived in rundown apartments and buildings along narrow city streets. People called these areas Japantowns.

Many Japanese immigrant men worked as farm laborers. Others found jobs in lumber camps, railroad camps, and factories. Men and women also found work as servants for wealthy families in western states.

Americans began to treat the Japanese immigrants badly. Japanese were not allowed to own land. Some shop owners would not sell goods to Japanese immigrants. Many cities restricted the areas where Japanese Americans could live.

17

SURVIVING IN AMERICA

"We have cast our lot with California. We are drifting farther and farther away from the traditions and ideas of our native country. Our sons and daughters do not know them at all. They do not care to know them. They regard America as their home."

—George Shima, Japanese American farmer, 1920

Throughout the late 1800s and early 1900s, Japanese immigrants found work in agriculture. Many continued to work on the Hawaiian plantations. Others worked on farms in California and other western states. Some of these immigrant farm workers became sharecroppers. They worked on someone else's land and kept part of the crop to use or sell.

Japanese immigrants saved the money earned from sharecropping to buy their own farmland. They became successful farmers because they were able to grow crops on land that no one else wanted. In the hot, dry climate of California, Japanese farmers used farming techniques learned in Japan to make soil fertile. They grew a variety of fruits and vegetables, including strawberries, rhubarb, tomatoes, carrots, lettuce, asparagus, and cabbage.

Japanese American farmers were among the first in America to sell crops directly to consumers. Farmers and their families loaded up small trucks with their home-grown fruits and vegetables. They then drove to the city and sold their produce on street corners. They saved money because they did not have to pay someone else to bring their crops to a store. This truck farming style is similar to the farmers' markets found in American cities today.

Japanese immigrants made a living in other ways. Some worked in the fishing business. Japan is an island nation, and many immigrants had grown up learning how to fish in the old country. In America, they fished off the western coast. Japanese

immigrants also found jobs in the gold and silver mines of Utah or the coal mines of Colorado. Some went to work in lumber mills and logging camps.

At first, Americans were glad to see the Japanese immigrants arrive because businesses needed workers. But when the immigrants earned enough money to start their own businesses, other Americans saw them as a threat. Japanese Americans often ran small family businesses and did not hire other workers. Family members often worked without wages, making their cost to do business lower. Japanese Americans then could afford to offer lower prices on their goods and services. Some business owners were afraid of losing profits if they competed with Japanese Americans.

Many Japanese immigrants worked on California farms. They planted and harvested a variety of fruits and vegetables.

These photographs of a picture bride and her husband were attached to Department of Labor stationery for identification. In the early 1900s, thousands of Japanese women came to the United States as picture brides.

On February 18, 1907, the U.S. government and Japan passed the Gentleman's Agreement. This act limited the number of male Japanese immigrants allowed to enter the United States. Under the terms of this agreement, Japan stopped issuing passports to citizens who made their living as laborers. This agreement slowed Japanese immigration to America.

Japanese women were not included in the terms of the Gentleman's Agreement. Women still were allowed to immigrate to Hawaii and the United States. Japanese American men took advantage of this situation by sending for brides from Japan.

The process of bringing Japanese women to America for marriage was called the picture bride system. This method was based on the Japanese custom of parents arranging a marriage partner for their son or daughter. Under the picture bride system, a Japanese American man mailed his photo to a matchmaker in Japan. That person chose a bride for the man and sent back a photo of her. If both agreed to marry, the woman would sail to America to meet her new husband. From 1908 to 1924, thousands of Japanese women arrived in Hawaii and the United States as picture brides.

As more immigrants arrived in the United States and did well, other Americans began to envy them. Officials passed laws to keep immigrants from being successful. In

Japanese women were allowed to enter the United States and Hawaii as immigrants even after Japanese men were limited entry in 1907.

1913, the California legislature passed a law that prevented anyone born in another country from applying for U.S. citizenship or owning land in California.

The U.S. legislature also passed a series of laws against immigrants. The Immigration Act of 1917 also was known as the Barred Zone Act. This law did not allow immigrants from certain areas of Asia, such as Japan and China, to come to the United States.

Throughout the 1920s, U.S. lawmakers saw immigrants as a threat to other citizens. In 1921, they introduced an act that limited immigrants from each country into the United States. In 1922, the U.S. Supreme Court ruled that Japanese immigrants could not become U.S. citizens. This decision prevented Japanese immigrants from voting or running for political office. In 1924, the U.S. legislature passed the Asian Exclusion Act. Immigrants from Asian countries were not allowed to apply for U.S. citizenship.

Many Americans were angered by the Japantowns forming in large cities. They refused to sell land or homes to Japanese immigrants. But they also accused Japanese immigrants of resisting the American way of life. Many citizens did not want Japanese American children to go to public school with other children. As a result, Japanese Americans lived their lives together but separate from the rest of U.S. society.

DETENTION CAMPS

In 1942, detention camps opened to house Japanese Americans. They lived here in long, narrow buildings and were supervised by guards.

By the 1930s, many Japanese Americans were becoming accepted by others in the United States. They celebrated Independence Day with other Americans. They sent their children to school to learn English, American history, and other subjects. They worked and paid taxes.

On December 7, 1941, life changed for Japanese Americans. On that day, the Japanese Navy bombed the U.S. naval base at Pearl Harbor in Hawaii. This attack led the United States to enter World War II (1939–1945).

Americans became suspicious of Japanese Americans living along the West Coast. Some people thought those of Japanese background were spies or might send secret messages to friends and relatives in Japan. People wanted Japanese Americans removed from the West Coast, even though these people obeyed the law and remained loyal to the U.S. government.

On February 19, 1942, President Franklin Roosevelt signed Executive Order 9066. This command allowed the U.S. Army to remove Japanese Americans from their homes along the West Coast. It paved the way for the army to place them in detention camps under the watch of armed guards.

The U.S. government set up 10 detention camps. They were located in Colorado, Arkansas, Arizona, Wyoming, California, Idaho, and Utah. Workers built the camps quickly,

Until they were sent to detention camps in 1942, Japanese American children attended public schools. Like other children, they said the Pledge of Allegiance at school each day.

leaving many buildings without heat or indoor plumbing. Barbed wire and armed guards surrounded each camp. More than 120,000 Japanese Americans were forced to move to these detention camps.

Japanese American children went to school in the camps. Some graduated from high school there. Men and women grew crops in fields around the camps to provide food for the people who lived there.

By 1943, officials told the people they could leave the camps to join the U.S. Army, to attend school, or to work in the Midwest or on the East Coast. But many Japanese

Americans had given up their land and their businesses before entering the camps. Most young children and elderly people remained in the camps until the war ended. In 1945, the U.S. government closed the camps. But it was difficult for many Japanese Americans to start over with their lives.

In 1988, the U.S. government made an apology to every survivor of the detention camps. Congress voted to pay each survivor $20,000 to make amends for the injustice of the camps. In 1990, the U.S. government sent checks to the oldest survivors, along with an official letter of apology signed by President George Bush.

KEEPING TRADITIONS

Sushi is a favorite Japanese dish. It is made of raw fish, seaweed, vegetables, rice, and seasonings.

Today, Japanese Americans make up less than 1 percent of the U.S. population. Although their numbers are small, their contributions to American culture have been great.

Japanese Americans introduced new foods to America. The first Japanese American farmers found that California and Texas had ideal weather conditions for growing rice. Soon this grain became popular with people throughout the country. Sushi is a popular Japanese dish in the United States. Cooks mix rice with seasonings, vinegar, and water and spread it over a layer of seaweed. They then arrange strips of vegetables and raw fish over the rice. Finally, they roll the seaweed and ingredients into a long sausage shape and slice the sushi into bite-size pieces.

Family and religion remain important to Japanese Americans. It is common for three generations of a family to live together in the same home. Many Japanese Americans create their own ceremonies and traditions by combining parts of Christianity, Buddhism, and Shintoism. Christianity is a religion based on the life and teachings of Jesus, whom Christians believe is the son of God. Buddhists believe that people must work to be morally and mentally pure to be relieved of life's sufferings. The Shinto religion focuses on the belief that the Japanese emperor is a descendant of the sun goddess.

Many Japanese Americans have great respect for the arts. Japanese musicians play the koto, a Japanese stringed instrument that sounds similar to a harp. Artists

Kuri Kinton

★ ★

Kuri Kinton is a traditional Japanese dessert. Many Japanese Americans enjoy Kuri Kinton on special holidays such as New Year's Day.

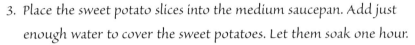

What You Need

Ingredients:

3 medium sweet potatoes

water (to cover sweet potatoes in saucepan)

½ cup (125 mL) sugar

½ teaspoon (2 mL) salt

12 chestnuts (canned and cooked in syrup)*

¼ cup (50 mL) of canned chestnut syrup

1 tablespoon (15 mL) toasted black
   sesame seeds*

(*found in Asian markets)

Equipment:

vegetable peeler

knife

medium saucepan

colander

potato masher

measuring cup

measuring spoons

wooden spoon

strainer

liquid measuring cup

small serving bowls

What You Do

1. Peel the sweet potatoes with the
   vegetable peeler.

2. Cut the sweet potatoes into ½-inch
   (1.3-centimeter) slices.

3. Place the sweet potato slices into the medium saucepan. Add just
   enough water to cover the sweet potatoes. Let them soak one hour.

4. Cook sweet potatoes in the saucepan over medium heat for 20 minutes or
   until sweet potatoes are tender.

5. Place a colander in the sink and drain the sweet potatoes.

6. Return the sweet potatoes to the saucepan and use the potato masher to
   mash them.

7. Add sugar and salt to sweet potatoes.

8. Place the strainer over the liquid measuring cup. Allow the syrup from the
   canned chestnuts to drain into the measuring cup. Pour out all but ¼ cup
   (50 mL) of the syrup.

9. Stir ¼ cup (50 mL) of the syrup into the mashed sweet potatoes.

10. Gently mix drained chestnuts into the mashed sweet potatoes.

11. Spoon two to three chestnuts into a bowl. Mound mashed sweet potatoes
    over each chestnut.

12. Sprinkle toasted black sesame seeds over the Kuri Kinton and serve.

Makes four to six servings

This Japanese dancing doll is displayed as a decoration on most days. But on March 3, Japanese American girls display a special set of imperial court dolls called Hina sama.

often practice sumi-e, the Japanese art of brush painting. Artists use special brushes and strokes to create sumi-e paintings. Other artists practice origami, the Japanese art of paper folding. Origami artists create animal shapes and other forms from single squares of paper. The Japanese consider flower arranging an art. They call their special type of flower arranging ikebana. Artists create beautiful flower arrangements using only a few branches, leaves, or flowers to represent the heavens, humans, and Earth.

Many Japanese Americans continue to celebrate traditional festivals. One of the most important festivals is Oshogatsu, or Japanese New Year, on January 1. Japanese Americans celebrate New Year's with family gatherings. Cooks prepare Japanese fish called tai for the festivities. On New Year's Eve, people eat long, thick noodles called soba, which stand for long life. They also enjoy a dish made with sweet rice balls called mochi. Mochi are a sign of good fortune to the Japanese.

Two special holidays honor Japanese boys and girls. On March 3, Japanese Americans celebrate Hina Matsuri, the Girls' Day festival. Families honor daughters on this day. On May 5, Japanese Americans celebrate Tango No Sekku. Families celebrate this Boys' Day festival to wish their sons a good future. Family members traditionally hang carp-shaped kites or wind socks from a flagpole in their yards.

Japanese Americans have blended into U.S. society. They enjoy life in many parts of the United States and they hold a variety of careers. Many are doctors, lawyers, scientists, and teachers. Others are musicians, artists, poets, actors, and athletes.

★ Make a Family Tree ★

Genealogy is the study of family history. Genealogists often record this history in the form of a family tree. This chart records a person's ancestors, such as parents, grandparents, and great-grandparents.

Start your own family tree with the names of your parents and grandparents. Ask family members for their full names, including their middle names. Remember that your mother and grandmothers likely had a different last name before they were married. This name, called a maiden name, is probably the same as their fathers' last name.

Making a family tree helps you to know your ancestors and the countries from which they emigrated. Some people include the dates and places of birth with each name on their family tree. Knowing when and where these relatives were born will help you understand from which immigrant groups you have descended.

There are many ways to find information for your family tree. Ask for information from your parents, grandparents, and as many other older members of your family as you can. Some people research official birth and death records to find the full names of relatives. Genealogical societies often have information that will help with family tree research. If you know the cemetery where family members are buried, you may find some of the information you need on the gravestones.

Your father's mother

Your father's father

Your mother's father

Your father

Your mother's mother

Your mother

You

★ TIMELINE ★

1600

1633
Japanese laws do not allow foreigners to enter the country. Japanese citizens are not allowed to leave.

1853
Commodore Matthew C. Perry arrives in Japan. His military forces convince Japanese officials to open Japan to trade with other countries.

1800

1868
The emperor allows Japanese citizens to leave the country. Japanese immigration to Hawaii begins.

1882
The U.S. government passes the Chinese Exclusion Act, which stops Chinese immigrants from entering the country. Japanese immigrants begin coming to the U.S. mainland looking for work.

1900

1900
Hawaii becomes a U.S. territory under the Organic Act. Plantation owners no longer are allowed to hire workers under labor contracts.

1922
The U.S. Supreme Court rules that Japanese immigrants are not eligible to become U.S. citizens.

1942
President Franklin Roosevelt signs Executive Order 9066, setting into motion the forced removal of Japanese Americans into detention camps.

1941
The Japanese Navy bombs the U.S. naval base at Pearl Harbor in Hawaii. America declares war on Japan and enters World War II (1939–1945).

1945
World War II ends and detention camps close. Japanese Americans return to their former homes in the West. Many have already moved to midwestern or eastern states.

1988
The U.S. government officially apologizes to every survivor of the detention camps. Congress votes to pay each survivor $20,000 to make amends for the injustice of the camps.

Patsy Takemoto Mink (1927–) Mink was born in Paia, Hawaii. She was the first Japanese American woman to become a lawyer in Hawaii. She also was the first Japanese Nisei woman elected to the U.S. House of Representatives.

Nonyuki "Pat" Morita (1932–) Morita was born in Iselton, California. Morita worked as a computer operator, disc jockey, actor, and comedian. In 1985, he was nominated for an Academy Award for his movie role as Mr. Miyagi in *The Karate Kid*. He also played Arnold on the TV show *Happy Days*.

Yoko Ono (1933–) Ono is a Japanese American artist who was born in Tokyo, Japan. She and her family moved to the United States in 1951. She married John Lennon, who once was a member of the band The Beatles.

Yoko Ono

George Takei (1939–) Takei was born in Los Angeles. He is an actor best known for his role as Commander Sulu in the *Star Trek* TV series and movies. Takei also serves on the boards of many civic and cultural groups, including the Japanese American National Museum in Los Angeles.

Kristi Yamaguchi (1971–) Yamaguchi was born in Hayward, California. She began skating lessons when she was 5 years old and entered her first skating competition at age 8. Yamaguchi is the first Japanese American woman to win an Olympic gold medal for ice skating. She won her medal at the 1992 Olympic Games.

Kristi Yamaguchi

Words to Know

Buddhism (BOO-diz-uhm)—a religion based on the teaching of Buddha; Buddhists believe that you live many lives in different bodies.

Christianity (kriss-chee-AN-uh-tee)—the religion based on the life and teachings of Jesus; Christians believe that Jesus is the son of God and that he died so that, after death, people's souls would go to heaven.

culture (KUHL-chur)—a way of life, ideas, customs, and traditions of a certain group of people

emigrant (EM-uh-gruhnt)—a person who leaves his or her own country in order to live in another country

exclusion (ek-SKLOO-shun)—the act of keeping some people out of a group

foreigner (FOR-uhn-er)—someone who is from another country

immigrant (IM-uh-gruhnt)—a person who comes to another country to live permanently

immunize (IM-yuh-nize)—to protect someone from catching a disease

matchmaker (MACH-may-kur)—a person who arranges to bring two unmarried people together for marriage

plantation (plan-TAY-shuhn)—a large farm found in warm climates; crops such as pineapples and sugar were grown on plantations in Hawaii.

Shintoism (SHIN-toh-isuhm)—the main religion of Japan that involves the worship of ancestors and the spirits of nature

shogun (SHOH-goon)—military governors who once ruled Japan

To Learn More

Alonso, Karen. *Korematsu v. United States: Japanese-American Internment Camps.* Landmark Supreme Court Cases. Springfield, N.J.: Enslow, 1998.

Blumberg, Rhoda. *Shipwrecked!: The True Adventures of a Japanese Boy.* New York: HarperCollins, 2000.

Cooper, Michael L. *Fighting for Honor: Japanese Americans and World War II.* New York: Clarion Books, 2000.

Krasno, Rena. *Floating Lanterns and Golden Shrines: Celebrating Japanese Festivals.* Berkeley, Calif.: Pacific View Press, 2000.

Welch, Catherine A. *Children of the Relocation Camps.* Picture the American Past. Minneapolis: Carolrhoda Books, 2000.

Places to Write and Visit

Four Rivers Cultural Center and Museum
676 SW Fifth Avenue
Ontario, OR 97914

Japanese American National Museum
369 East First Street
Los Angeles, CA 90012-3901

Japanese American World War II Library
16907 Brighton Avenue
Gardena, CA 90247

Japanese Canadian National Museum and Archives Society
#120 – 6688 Southoaks Crescent
Burnaby, BC V5E 4M7 Canada

Manzanar National Historic Site
661 North Edwards Street, P.O. Box 426
Independence, CA 93526-0426

National Japanese American Historical Society
1684 Post Street
San Francisco, CA 94115-3604

Internet Sites

Japan through Young Eyes
http://www.wnn.or.jp/wnn-tokyo/english/young/001

Japanese American History Archives
http://www.amacord.com/fillmore/museum/jt/jaha/jaha.html

JIN Kids Web Japan
http://jin.jcic.or.jp/kidsweb

National Japanese American Historical Society
http://www.njahs.org

A Short Chronology of Japanese American History
http://www.janet.org/janet_history/niiya_chron.html

Index